"Who Am I"

"Who Am I?"

a Christian, Biblical Introduction to Gender Identity for Young Boys

Candice Mary Thomas

Published by DTJ Press

Copyright © 2022 Candice Mary Thomas

Images designed by Freepik, www.Freepik.com.

No part of this book may be reproduced or transmitted in any form or by an means, electronic or mechanical, including photocopying and recording, or by any information storage or retrieval system, except as may be expressly permitted in writing by the author. Requests for permission should be emailed to dtjpress@gmail.com.

ISBN: 978-1-7332133-9-4

Printed in the United States of America.

Dedicated to ALL boys!

You are made uniquely and specially in the image of God! He formed every cell in your body to be who you are. May you be blessed as you find your true identify in Him and in who He made you to be!

Who am I? When I look in the mirror, I see a boy, but some boys call me a **sissy**. Does that mean I'm not supposed to be a boy, but that I'm a girl?

Mom and Dad say I'm a boy, but is that true?

I don't like karate . . .

wrestling . . .

Fencing . . . **OR**

boxing . . .

I don't like building things . . .

and I don't want to grow up to do construction work.

I'd rather dance!

I love hip-hop!

jazz . . .

. . . but my favorite is ballet!

One day I want to dance like Mikhail Baryshnikov!

I love cooking . . .

baking . . .

and even playing dolls with my sister and her friends.

I am so confused! I sometimes think being a girl might be who I really am, but would that be right?

Mom and Dad are at work, so I decide to walk next door to my Nonni and Papa's house and ask questions. They have lots of answers, but Papa says that's because he reads the Bible, and it is God who has all of the answers.

Nonni answers my knock. "Well, well," she says with a twinkle in her eyes. "I can tell it's hot chocolate and cookie time! Come on in!"

Off she goes to heat the chocolate milk and grab some of her famous peanut butter cookies. I can always count on Nonni for treats, and I love to help her bake them!

I walk in and stand near Papa. "I'm so confused," I say. "Today my teacher had each of us tell what name we wanted to be called and whether we thought we were a boy, a girl, or other.

Then she said if we weren't sure, we should talk to her. She could refer us to somone who would give us medicine that would slow the growth of girls into women and boys into men.

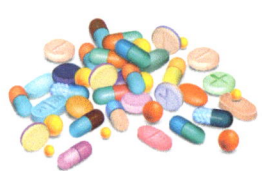

This would give us time to decide, and our parents didn't need to know. It would be a secret! Mom and Dad have always taught me not to have secrets.

I'm all mixed up, Papa, and I don't understand!
Am I a boy **OR** am I a girl?
What do you think? "

"Come over here and sit on my lap," says Papa. "Well, now," he continues, "what I think is not really important, but it is very important to know what God thinks!" Papa picks up his Bible. It is always on the table near him. He opens it up close to the beginning and tells me to read along with him in the book of Genesis. We read all the way through the first chapter. I learn that when God created living things--birds and sea creatures--He created them according to their kinds, and God said this was good!

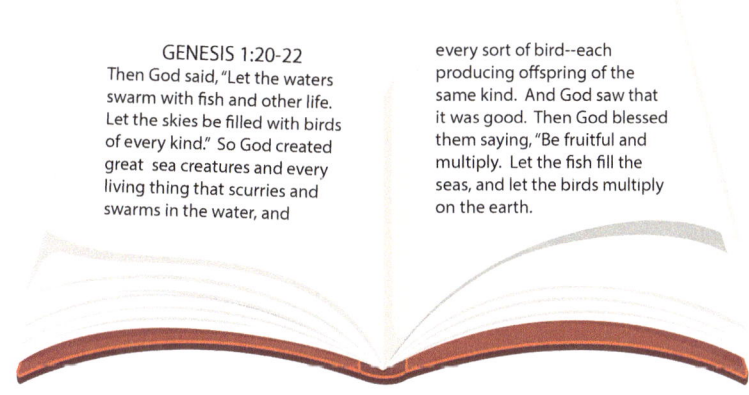

GENESIS 1:20-22
Then God said, "Let the waters swarm with fish and other life. Let the skies be filled with birds of every kind." So God created great sea creatures and every living thing that scurries and swarms in the water, and every sort of bird--each producing offspring of the same kind. And God saw that it was good. Then God blessed them saying, "Be fruitful and multiply. Let the fish fill the seas, and let the birds multiply on the earth.

God saw that everything was good!

Then He created livestock . . .

crawling creatures . . .

and wildlife . . .

. . . everything according to its kinds, and He said this was good.

"According to their kinds . . . Does this mean that monkeys are monkeys and men are men and that men did not come from monkeys like some people say?" I ask.

"That's exactly right," says Papa. "It means that a fish will never become an alligator, and a monkey will never bccome a man."

**A FISH IS A FISH
AND
THAT'S ALL
A FISH WILL EVER BE!**

Papa once more reads toward the end of Genesis 1. " 'So God created **human beings** in **His own image**. **In the image of God** He created them; **male and female** He created them.' **Genesis 1:27** So you see," says Papa, "God made men to be men, women to be women; girls to be girls, and boys to be boys. We are all made in His image according to His perfect design!"

**This is God's design:
THAT
BOYS grow into MEN . . .**

AND

GIRLS grow into WOMEN.

Nonni is back now. She hands me my hot chocolate and a cookie, then picks up the clay vase I gave her one Christmas.

"Remember making this?" Nonni asks.

"Sure," I say. "I had to do it over and over and over! Finally I thought it was just right."

"So," explains Nonni, "as the vase's creator, you had the right to judge it. You had a design in mind for its purpose . . . to hold water and flowers . . . and you wanted it to be be a color I love. Right?"

"That's right." I take the vase from Nonni and hold it carefully in my hands. It now has beautiful, colorful daisies in it. "It does everything I wanted. It holds water, is your favorite color, and it is more beautiful than ever with God's daisies in it!"

Nonni laughs. "God always has a way of making things better!"

"And just like you judged your creation, God judged His!" Papa adds. "Do you remember what He said?"

"He said everything was good," I reply.

"Yes, and after He made mankind **male** and **female** and looked over His entire creation, He said everything was ***VERY, VERY GOOD!***"

Papa explains once more, "Men and women, boys and girls--that was and is our Creator's design, and His words tell us He was very pleased with that!"

"This makes sense," I say, "but what about me? How do I know He didn't goof when He made me? I look like a boy, but sometimes I feel like a girl, and I always want to do girl things."

"Am I a girl OR a boy? That is the question."

Nonni hands me another cookie. I begin to eat it, dunking its sugary sweetness in my hot chocolate first.

"Grandson," she says. "Let me read to you something from another book of the Bible." She takes the Bible from Papa's hands and tells me she is turning to Psalm 139. She reads me verses 13-16, explaining to me that a man after God's own heart, David, wrote the words. She reads, " *'For You created my inmost being. You knit me together in my mother's womb. I praise You because I am fearfully and wonderfully made; Your works are wonderful, I know that full well. My frame was not hidden from You when I was made in the secret place, when I was woven together in the depths of the earth. Your eyes saw my unformed body; all the days ordained for me were written in Your book before one of them came to be.'* "

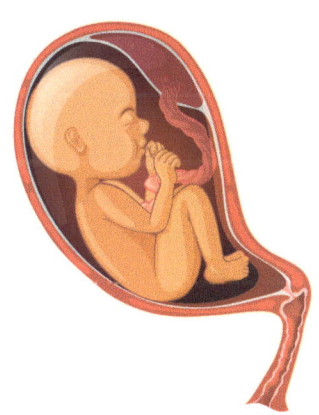

God had a special design for David's life, and He formed David's body for that purpose.

Nonni continues, "God gave David these words to help him understand who God made him to be, but God also means them for you and me and for everyone He creates! God had a design--a plan--for who He would make you to be. He made you that way to fulfill your life's purpose!!"

"Get it?" asks Papa. "God knit you together stich by stitch, and after He created you, He broke the mold. **He made you special**--one of a kind--in His image. With one stitch He made

a boy who loves to dance; with another, to cook and bake; and with another, to play dolls with your sister and her friends. When God knit you together, He created a very creative, loving, and compassionate boy, and one day you will be a most understanding man!

"So you see," Papa continues, **"it's not how you feel or your interests that define whether you are a boy or girl; it is your body!** Precious boy, Nonni and I are thrilled with who God made you to be, and we would have you no other way! Now," says Papa, "finish those cookies and let's go . . . I want you to teach me how to bake!"

Papa slowly gets up from his chair. "Hurry up, Papa!" I say as I dance pirouettes into the kitchen. "Set the oven to 350 degrees. This is going to be **soooo** much fun!"

Who am I? I am a special, unique boy, who is made in the image of God. I love many things like dancing, cooking, baking, and playing dolls . . . and that's okay. How do I know? I know because that's how God created me, and God doesn't make mistakes!

"I'm glad I'm a boy. Thank you, Father!"

Dear God,

Thank You for being my Heavenly Father and for teaching me the truth of who I am through Your Holy Word, the Bible. You designed me in Your image and knit each part of me according to Your loving purpose for my life.

I understand that You created me to be a boy. Thank You! Now I look forward to discovering what you've planned for my future as a man. Help me always to honor You in my words and actions, and may others be blessed because of who You made me to be, your special son!

Jesus, you gave me eternal life when I asked You to be my Savior, and I love you with all my heart, soul, and mind. Thank You, and help me always to shine for You!

Your amazing and loving son . . .

_____.

(Your name)

Who is Jesus?

Have you heard about Jesus? Do you know who He is and what He did for you and for me--for everyone? Well, we had better start at the beginning.

Imagine there being nothing. No time, no universe, no earth, no creature, no man, no woman…nothing. But there was something…**SOMETHING GREAT AND MIGHTY**, something more than we can ever imagine, and that was our triune God! Triune means three, so our triune God is one God with three persons, and before time, the persons were the Father, the Word, and the Holy Spirit—a **TRUE MYSTERY** to our human minds!

Now God is love, and that love was so great, God wanted to share it. So God created day and night, the sun and moon, and there was time! Then He created everything we see and know, including the first man and woman, Adam and Eve. He placed them in the Garden of Eden and gave them everything they needed for life: a perfect climate, food, fields to cultivate (yes, work is important, bringing us great satisfaction!), and a close love relationship with Him.

There is one thing God did not want, however, and that was robots who had no choice but to love Him! So God gave Adam and Eve free will. They could choose to always remain close to Him by obeying what He asked of them, or they could choose to disobey and be separated from Him for all time. You probably know the story here. Adam and Eve did rebel against their Father by doing the one thing He asked them *never* to do; they ate the fruit from the tree of knowledge of good and evil. With that act, sin entered the world, and *all humans* throughout all time thereafter *inherited that sin nature*, which means that *we are naturally drawn to sin and rebellion against God*. By that act, Adam and Eve were permanently separated from God, as all mankind would be forever.

God, however, loved mankind too much to let this happen! He wants us with Him forever! So God needed a perfect man, one who would not sin, to take the sins of others upon Himself to end that gap of separation. The only one who could be that perfect was God Himself, so He sent the Word (*the second person of the Holy Trinity)* to come into our world as His only begotten Son, a baby, who would be named Jesus.

As a baby, God's FORM changed from the Word to that of a man, but His nature did not! He remained God always, pure and sinless. ANOTHER MYSTERY! So this baby, Jesus Christ, grew into a man, and because He remained pure and sinless, God was able to accept His sacrifice on the cross in our place. What does this mean? Jesus defeated sin by taking all sins since the beginning of time and throughout all future times upon Himself! He suffered, died, was buried, then rose from the dead. Can you imagine a greater love than this?

When we confess our sins to God and ask Jesus to be our Savior, we immediately become God's children and His Holy Spirit *(the third person of the Holy Trinity)* enters us. **Our form (our body) remains the same, but we have an entirely new nature!** It's a **THIRD MYSTERY**, because when we look in the mirror, we look the same! However, we are now new creations with a new nature that desires to sin less and less and, through the strength of the Holy Spirit in us, we grow in goodness and become more like Christ. This is fantastic, but we must know that we never can do enough good things to earn our way to heaven. It is Jesus' sacrifice and claiming Him as our Savior that allows us to live forever with God in the peace, love, and joy He always intended for us.

Have you ever asked Jesus to take away your sins and be your Savior? If not, now is the perfect time to ask Him! Use your own words, read aloud the prayer below, or repeat the following words after someone else reads them to you:

Prayer for Salvation

Jesus, I confess that I willfully make wrong choices over and over--that I sin--and I know that without You I am lost. I know that because of Your amazing love, You died in my place on the cross, were buried, then rose from the dead. Today, I ask You to forgive me of all my sins, past, present, and future, and to be my Savior. With Your Holy Spirit living in me, I know I will grow to be a boy who is more and more like You each day. I look forward to this and to living with You forever in heaven! Thank You for Your great sacrifice and for loving me so very much! YOU ARE THE BEST!! Amen. *Your name_____ Today's date_____*

*If you have found this book of value,
I would love for you to write an online review
on Amazon, Goodreads, etc. Thank you!*

ALSO AVAILABLE FOR YOUNG GIRLS:

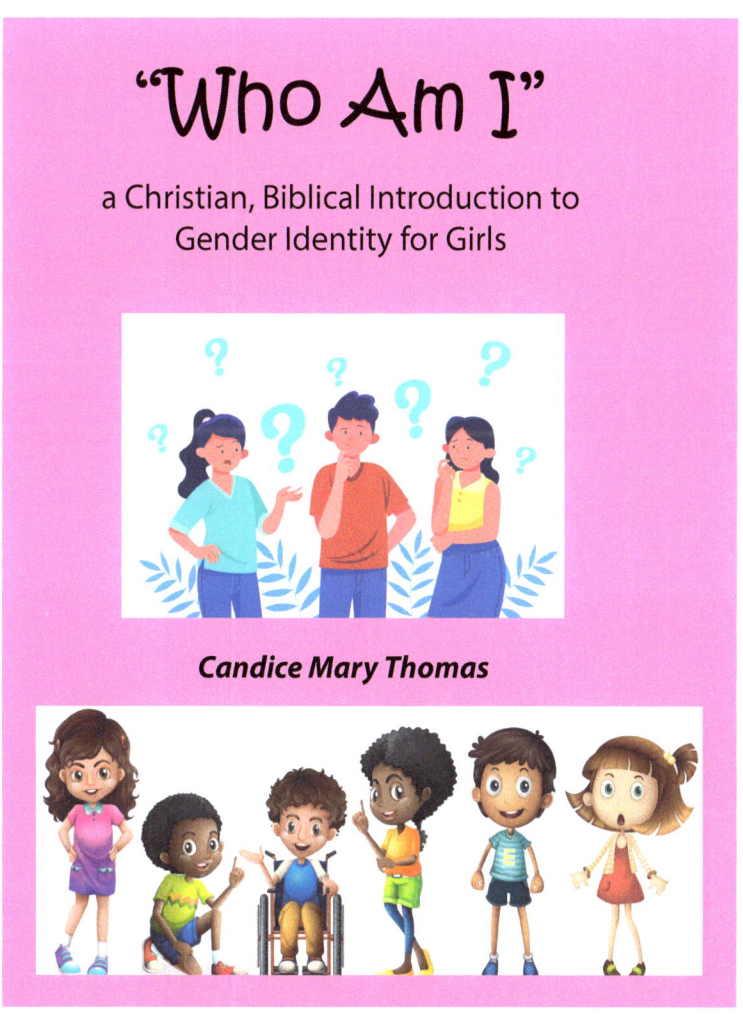

OTHER WORKS BY CANDICE MARY THOMAS

BIBLE STUDIES FOR TEENS
Jesus' Words for Teens: Obedience
Jesus' Words for Teens: Standing Tall
(Both with Leader's Guides and Teen Workbooks)

  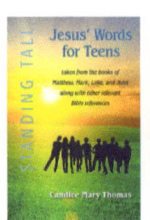 

CHILDREN'S FICTION

Granny Mae Saves the Day
Join Granny in this zany adventure as Granny and her little white dog, Bam Bam, chase down two silly bank robbers.

COMING SOON!

Granny Mae Meets Harry P. Best (and the Walapazoo!)

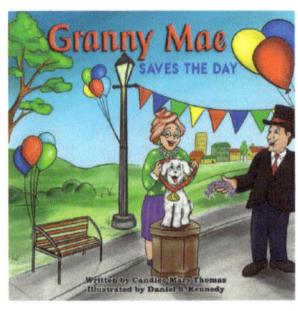 

WEEKLY WEDNESDAY DEVOTIONS

Join Candice every Wednesday at
www.candicemarythomas.com for a devotional.
Use the contact form to join her email list.

Find out more about
Candice Mary Thomas on her website:
www.candicemarythomas.com